Slovenia
My Country

Photographs Joco Žnidaršič
Introductory text Milan Kučan
Accompanying text Željko Kozinc
Layout Miljenko Licul

Joco Žnidaršič

Slovenia
My Country

Veduta

J oco Žnidaršič has an unusual book coming out. After so many of them, in which he has merged his artistic perceptions, this book about Slovenia simply had to materialise. It has taken a long time to mature, and now it is amongst us with an utterly original image of Slovenia, with its four images, in fact, different to those to which our eyes have got accustomed to through the matrix of the experience of life. Earth, water, wood and stone. Yes, this is Slovenia; this, too, is Slovenia. It can be seen and experienced in this way as well, and this will surely be confirmed by everybody who is acquainted with our Slovene country in somewhat greater detail. These pictures seem so well-known when looking at them, gathered in Žnidaršič's book. Seen so many times and again just recently; somewhere. It is difficult to tell, however, exactly where and when, because they seem so familiar, so very ours that they could have been taken anywhere in our country and at any time. On these images, virtually no people can be seen. But they are still there. As if they went off on some errand for a moment or two. "And what are people other than wood and fallow and soil?" wrote long ago the Carinthian Dr Fran Sušnik, one of the most susceptible judges of Slovenia and the human soul of its inhabitants. People and epochs expire, a mountain remains, for ever.

A lot of walking was needed across Slovenia to get such images of hers. First of all they had to ripen in the soul. The eye and the lens merely searched for them. To look for and to focus in places where it seemed that they had to be there anyway - as specifically emphasised little stones in the mosaic of the image of that place. In such shape, Slovenia has to be experienced in different seasons and in different hours of the day. You have to be patient with her, feel her. And above all, you have to love her. So very much that you can accept the following truth: from people you take leave easier than from soil. With each of these images, Joco Žnidaršič takes leave from soil. But only until its next image. The image of soil with a message intended for people. Those who have walked across Slovenia with love, experienced all of her unusual forms and are now carrying them in their hearts. Joco is only reminding us of them. He caught the memory into a moment, which he is now offering to us.

Milan Kučan

Earth is like love. Something soft, like hope, for when looking at it, it sinks into its soul and perseveres there totally speechless, although it would love to utter a word or even sing. We are struck by the wish to live rooted in it, like an evergreen, as we wish to be safe, firm and strong, spiritually nourished. For earth is subjected to us, kind to us, quiet, durable and tenacious, even when we fatefully poke into its motherly patience. The earth of Slovenia, seemingly tranquil after numerous geological dramas in the last few millions of years, an eternal virgin penetrated by volcanoes, hurricanes, thunders, floods, scorching heat and plough, is again and again unveiled in front of us, it is summoning our intrepidity and consecration, our cry and laughter, our benevolence. Although it is the actual source of life, it needs our life's help; it needs our faith in ourselves, faith that we belong to it. It is looking for its future, just we ourselves are looking for it, this common fate. It prefers a deadlock than development, for we try to vitiate our nourisher with destructive means, by demolishing the old consents as to its beauty and justice. It depends on our state of mind whether it shall remain balanced in its natural processes. It needs healthy seeds not merely for its furrows but also for tranquillity in its calm parts. Only in this way can it remain home to animals that have adapted to it better than man, can become a refuge for people in secludedness and displacement, the two ever increasing forces. Only in this way can it remain a well-being to those for whom it procreates and to those on whose sources of energy it renews its strength. A look at domestic earth always entices our love to unyielding, unconditional loyalty.

The young birch trees of Bela krajina in a light mist and the young vineyard poles of the Vipava Valley in a warm evening zephyr: Bela krajina and the Vipava Valley are just two of the numerous little Slovene provinces, each distinguished for its unique nature. All of them eloquently speak of the most diverse geological, soil, water and climatic conditions in our country. Due to this heterogeneousness, Slovenia is known for its exceptional biodiversity, one of the highest in Europe and the world. The two photographs depict, on the one hand, the old cultural landscape full of plant and animal habitats, and, on the other

hand, the modern rural landscape, where only a single plant is allowed to prosper, where people are ordered to live fast, in accordance with the market profit principles. A grove to the right, where an agronostalgic person would spur a horse if anybody would be prepared to look after the animal, and furrows above, which can be negotiated only by tractor if anybody would be capable of handling it there. Hedgerows, ferns, mushrooms, butterflies, a true mental pabulum, to the right, and bare soil, tamed with herbicides, the place of work and extortionate growing processes, above; a birdless land, a workshop of the godly fertilisers. Which place is better, which one more valuable?

On previous pages: *Springtime in the fields spreading along the fertile Sava river alluvial deposits below the Kamnik-Savinja Alps.*

The cherries of Goriška Brda and the Vipava Valley (two small photographs below) are impatiently violating the average Slovene time of bloom during the vernal equinox characteristic of the Dolenjska (larger photograph on the left) or Kozjansko (smaller photograph on the top) regions. At that time the white Aries of the zodiac procreates, in meadows and riverine woodlands, its innumerable children. Trees become a booming sign of the primeval nature and warmth, fragile and short-lived as happiness. The days bathe in the little crowns of whiteness, the earth is celebrating its wedding, and the brown tongues of fertility are already creeping across its soil. In spring, the tongues are still learning the language of fruits.

On previous pages: *If the stars glittered only above Slovenia, the entire world would rush to this country. Something similar is happening to the daffodil, our cultic plant. In nature it prospers only on the slopes of Golica in the Karavanke Mountains, which is the reason why each May it attracts thousands of its admirers to its blooming fields. The plant's white veils, pierced with the yellow dots of dandelions, address the people's exhausted hearts as a special gift of spring. Daffodil is a mysterious flower, as testified by one of our stories. Namely, bees were punished as they had not respected the Lord's Day and gathered honey on Sundays. Immediately under their blossoms the Lord made little knots and thus locked the sweet sap in them. And this is the reason why daffodils are called "locks" by the locals.*

If a farmer was asked to pick and choose between sense and stout potatoes, he would have certainly opted for the latter. And this certainly is sense. Potato, a perennial with edible tuberous roots grown as a pot plant less than three centuries ago, became one of the most widely spread arable crops in the continental part of Slovenia, particularly in the alluvial deposits of the Sava river below Mt. Storžič (right), where brown and with pebbles well mixed soil, a true paradise for the potato, had been formed. The farmer used sense to make the potato stouter, and he was also sensible enough to gave it about thirty

different Slovene names. Slovene agricultural experts, on the other hand, have brought up 14 different potato varieties and gave them some nice brotherly and sisterly names, such as Igor, Yana, Jake, Daisy and Anthony. Well, the exaggerated forcing of the potato to become even stouter has clearly not been the best thing to do, for in Slovenia it has somehow vitiated and is no longer as good as it used to be… Perhaps we should ask St. Jacob, the patron saint of arable crops and the old folk intercessor for the good sun, to provide us with some sense, or perhaps make a pilgrimage to his little church in the Polhov Gradec Dolomites, so gorgeously placed on the top of a bear hill, as shown by the smaller photograph.

Vine must catch as much sun as possible. This is why the forefathers of our winegrowers, even the ancient Romans, used to grow them in lines on sunward slopes. Such vine is still being planted here and there at Haloze (smaller photograph in the middle), home to the best quality white wines such as Riesling, Rizvaner and Roulander, and in the Dolenjska region (below), home to the Slovene indigenous "Cviček", also called "The Reddish Lad" (as originally named by Tone Pavček, the Slovene poet). On the right we can see trellises standing near Branik in the Gorica area, the heavenly graceful land (as named by Simon Gregorčič, another Slovene poet), the land of Pinnella, Barbera and The Green, where the majority of vineyards are situated on terraces for easier cultivation and water retainment. The slopes and ridges strewn with wine terraces seem like huge sunflowers with which the earth is turning towards the sun. Everything procreated by the earth and the sun is an inexhaustible pot of abundance from which wine flows as from a spring. In the venerable earthen pot on which vine, as an ancient symbol of the tree of life (larger photograph), is depicted lies the treasure of the ancient dream supplied by the riches of the earth.

There's no nicer girl than a female reaper, there's no nicer cereal than the wheat. There's no nicer weed than this poppy of Bela krajina, and there's no nicer sweetmeat than the Prekmurje gibanica, which with its purple layer of poppy seeds takes away from this plant some of the opiate weed ill repute. Poppy ripens quickly, and its fragile beauty burns fast as well. But in its seed, so small than only the people in the moment of total humbleness are smaller than them, remains the power of sleep and oblivion, the power of death and resurrection.

On previous pages: *The fertile collapse dolina on the Gora above the Vipava Valley. When reached by the stormy winds coming from the sea, they are usually accompanied by heavy rain, which eventually fills this cave- and sieve-like place with no streams at all. Plants and animals must make haste to consume this gift, for the Gora drought is inexorable and impatient.*

*At the moment when a play of two lights
intertwines above Štorje in the Karst
and above Mt. Nanos (larger
photograph) and when mist (smaller
photographs) bestows its fugacious
alchemy on itself at the Ljubljana
Marshes, the sun and the moon play like
children with the Marshes' deer and
birds. Our own heart becomes unknown
to us, and the whirls of our wishes are
suddenly with no direction at all, with
no master. But confidence still
inundates us with its sweet thought
on peace, the confidence which flows
between us and the world. We have
been drawn closer to it. This is a safe,
trustful merit of the late afternoon's
light. We begin to make a decision of
how we shall live. The sun and
the moon observe the valleys and
the mountains of our visual perception,
the sunset is still brisk, while the sunrise
is still drowsing in the sky, waiting
to send the stars to the great
nocturnal journey.*

Industrial oil plants, including rape, already cover no less than 2.5% of the Slovene fields. If on the one hand these plants are violating the earth, with the aid of various chemical preparations, by occupying the best soil (on photographs in the Dolenjska region and in the area of Slovenske gorice), they are leaving, on the other hand, an impression with their yellow carpets all over Slovenia that the earth is being inhabited by something new, which only seems joyful and only pretends to have borrowed light from the sun. Something similar can be said about dandelion, its yellow flowers and white inflorescence. Those potassium

and phosphoric mixtures, which have killed all those precious meadow flowers, are clearly very nourishing as far as dandelion is concerned. Shouldn't we ask ourselves what is happening to this paradise of ours? Isn't it true that due to the monocultures it is becoming very artificial and dull?

In former times, the Karst was known for its durable and loyal horses with firm bones and supple hooves, true children of the Karst land. In the 16th century, the Vienna emperor's horse breeders were struck by the idea to "marry" these horses with Spanish, Neapolitan and Arabic breeds, the most esteemed horses of that time. With the aid of the Karst people they reared a new breed of horses of very distinct and elegant appearance. They were named after Lipica, the place known for its healthy wind and Mediterranean sun, succulent pastures and shady oak groves. They eventually became court horses as well as Slovene holy animals

the taste of the Karst ponds, or imitate the perseverance of the Karst people even when bred outside their original home, like at Mavčiče in Sorško polje (smaller photograph below) or in Vrhnika near Lož (above).

that again and again inspired poets and the people overwhelmed with their beauty. The Lipica horses are born brown, black or grey, and only when six years old do they begin to change their colour into silky whiteness. Central Europe affords a number of Lipica horses stud farms, while Lipica itself is now renewing and restrengthening the reputation of its horse breeding origin. It has six lineages of original stallions (Pluto, Conversano, Neapolitano, Favory, Maestoso and Siglavy) and eighteen generations of brood mares. The Lipica horses show their bright nature, reflect the spirit of the Karst wind and

On previous pages: The traditional kozolec is a characteristic sign of the Slovene rural landscape, such as this one below Mt. Krvavec. The "embroidery" of fields, on the other hand, reveal our highly developed land culture. Can we at all imagine our cultural landscape without those field patterns, without a harmonious symbiosis of soil cultivation and the natural structure of the plots of land?

White colour unites all colours, while Bela krajina (smaller photograph in the middle) unites every characteristic of the Slovene land surface (Bela krajina literally meaning White landscape). As a landscape, however, it remains unique, from its customs and landscape images to the language spoken in it. Even the Bela krajina Karst differs from the Karst elsewhere in Slovenia, for example in Brkini (smaller photograph above) or in the Classical Karst, which is particularly beautiful, like in the area around Komen (photograph below) when the vineyards, which produce the Teran variety of grapes, turn red. The hilly and limestone country of the Dinaric part of Slovenia is everywhere embellished by birch groves with rich undergrowth of fern, which is in some village communities mown for livestock litter. Mowing and haymaking still joyfully reflect the rituals from the previous century, when associated with soil fertility. Today we look at such litter woodlands with nostalgia, as at paradise lost. Even buckwheat, here seen on the large photograph in the middle of the central Gorenjska plain, reminds of the yesterday world. In contrast to the fern it has triumphantly joined the new times of agriculture, when only one twentieth of the Slovene population still remains rural.

Wheat grows not only in Prekmurje, in the Dolenjska region or in the hills of Pohorje, where these photographs were made, but elsewhere in Slovenia, although not on every soil. Our forefathers chose to earmark for it only fields on the best sunward slopes or the best tended alluvial fields. Apart from it we have inherited from them, as tradition, the various warning wisdoms about bread as a source of live and survival. Like everywhere in the world, wheat is a nutrient beyond all comparison in our country as well, a selected cereal for various bread goodies, the basic farmer's obligation and blessing at the same time. It is not known where it originates from. Indeed, we can propagate different varieties of wheat, crossbreed them or improve their content value, but we can never create something parallel to it. Wheat is simply the gift of the sky, like life. Its grains and ears used to be the most valuable treasure of granaries and with their deep symbolism they became part of numerous poems, myths and even coats of arms.

Aren't these vine hills in Konjice, Haloze, Vipava Valley and the Karst (on smaller photographs) and particularly those around Lendava (on larger photograph) such as if combed by nymphs with different combs, but without coming to an agreement on where to do the partings? In places, the vineyards cut sharply or crookedly into each other, they adapt to the mechanical tilling, to new roads being built through them, to vineyard cottages being erected on the top of the ridges, and especially to the rolling land. The sea of vine hills is trying to calm down in all places and to straighten up as much as possible. It only wishes to be a fertile land friendly to man, sufficiently exposed to the sun, airy and moist for the best wines, such as Teran, The Green, Pinnella and Cviček, the truly autochthonous Slovene wines. Here it is interesting that the vine hills are situated mostly on the eastern and western margins of our country. A winegrower, who is a true artist in the creation of cultural landscape, unyieldingly persists on the ground on which wine had been produced even prior to the arrival of the Slavs. According to the data from the Geographical Atlas of Slovenia, a little more than 20,000 ha of land is covered with fertile vineyards with some 63 million vines, from which almost one hundred hectolitres of wine are produced.

According to the Italian poet Quasimodo, we all stand, on our own, on the top of the earth, pierced with the sun's ray, like this Istran reedmace (on larger photograph), like this pointed cloud, which wishes to be Mt. Storžič's brother, like these Notranjska hay-drying stakes, and like this Dolenjska kozolec (traditional Slovene hay rack). This is why we greedily take from the earth just everything we can reach, pick everything we wish, as if in our home garden (on previous two pages), even though the earth sometimes tries to resists us for it. Its colours are pleasing to our eyes, its tastes are opening our

hungry mouths. But our ears are still attentively listening to the earth's purpose, simply because we would like to be part of this purpose. We know that the purpose is coming from the sky, from the sun. We know that it contains our future. This is why we like it timidly, this earth, although we are greedy of its fruits, these symbols of the past and present. Earth is the deep and endless goal. Until the evening, which comes very quickly indeed.

On previous pages: Gartlc (garden), heavenly islet along a homestead at Dravsko polje

The setting sun above Ptujsko polje (larger photograph) fills us with the feeling that all those gaudy ribbons from the Korant's mask have been straightened and laid side by side in the narrow fields. The jerking, flaming red tongues, which awoke anxious unrest in us on Shrove Tuesday, have buried themselves in the autumn earth, and the droning shaking of the bells is now echoing only in our memory. Even the Korant's prickly stick wrapped with hedgehog's skin has fallen asleep in the last furrow of the upper part of the field. The Korant has done his job really well. Corn is trying to imitate his jumps and to paint, with the aid of the sun, its crowns gold. Sugar beet and potatoes are jostling for the space in the soil loosened by the Korants now dressed as peaceful farmers. Mist, the old vestal virgin of the plains, will soon lie down on the fields. The Korant's head will be wrapped by the soft white tuft full of rustling banknotes, made of irregularly shaped fields around homesteads, as well as of a cluster of fields cut up into long and narrow parallel patches.

St. John is looking at himself reflected in the mirror of Lake Bohinj, St. Daniel at Šentanel is exchanging glances with Mt. Uršlja, St. Michael at Pilštajn is a witness to the old fame of the Kozjansko stock fairs. St. Peter at Zavodnje is peering, with changeable luck, from the smog above the Šaleška valley... And here are also the triple churches in the Dolomites of Polhov Gradec, the constant apparitions in the mist on the larger photograph... On this page, however, we can see another three churches: from the regions of Gorenjska, Dolenjska and Bela krajina. But on thousand pages – if available to us – we could present images of yet another three thousand churches as believed to exist in Slovenia; and to each of them we could attribute its miraculous position in the country. One of them stands in an ancient, still pagan cultic place, the second guards the images of the portrayed people from the Middle Ages lent to the inhabitants of heaven, the third is a witness to the old apparitions of the Virgin... the fourth to a kind people's saint like St. Nicholas, the patron of no less than two hundred Slovene churches. Poverty was building walls, godfearing was constructing belfries, while the latter were lifting, from the earth, the sounds of their bells from the people to the Lord and vice versa.

On previous pages: Sinji vrh on the edge of the Trnovski gozd plateau, for millions of years folding above the Vipava Valley (with part of Vipava seen in the background). Here dramatically meet two of the Slovene worlds: the Dinaric and the Mediterranean ones. In this place you can often experience, at the very same time, a cold wind in your back and a warm breeze from the sea in your face.

At Spodnje Danje (left) and Sorica
(below) live descendants of the Škofja
Loka lords' subjects, who at the end
of the Middle Ages migrated, from
the places around the source of the
Drava river, to the sunward upland
wilderness just below Mt. Ratitovec.
At first, these sinewy men were clearing
forests for few consecutive years to
acquire some small fields and extensive
pastures, which still carry Slovenised
old names of generally known local
places. Then they brought their brides
or families with them. These villages,
the highest lying Slovene settlements,
bear witness, although strongly
depopulated, to yet another heroic

story about the settling of the Škofja
Loka mountains. The large sunny
glades with hamlets and isolated farms
have preserved amazingly beautiful
image of the cultivated upland rural
landscape, here and there quite rough
but, in the sun, quite gentle and softly
transforming world of peace and light
tranquillity. At a competition for
the most beautiful Slovene village – if
organised – Sorica could possibly win
the title.

On December 26th, St. Steven's Day, we can still watch here and there some dignified cavalcades. At Stara vas near Šentjur in the Dolenjska region (on the middle smaller photograph), for example, we can have a look at the so-called horse pilgrimage to the parish church. The horses are nicely attired, and at the head of the procession the house masters are riding in all their prominence. The young, who are allowed to follow them, are suppressing their briskness in the saddles, together with their little horses. They all encircle the church three times and attend a mass outside, during which the horses are blessed. The origin of this ritual dates to the distant past, and its tradition reaches back to Veles, the Slav God, worshipped around winter bonfires, when twelve wolf nights took place, during which the ghosts of the ancestors and the ghost of nature were tearing around people's homes. During the long winters, when people were telling each other most incredible stories, the ancestors were gazing at the stormy gallop of the mysterious Veles's horses. Christianity, persecuting the pagan aberrations, could not suppress the cult of horse as of a supernatural, magnificent being, and this is the reason why Christianity accepted the cult, although imposing certain features of humility on it. The horse monsters became submissive and loyal animals. But the time of the mythical winter story-telling still insists, in its last little parts, on some old rural provinces, such as Kozjansko (on larger photograph and on smaller photographs above) or Krško polje (smaller photograph below).

The village of Žrnjavec at Šavrinska brda as seen from afar.
In the foreground we can see the flysch bricks of a demolished house in the village of Topolovec.
On the gloomy sky above both hamlets a curtained light is flickering. Yet another motif of the abandoned Istra, said the scriber of light, so let's record it. And he pressed the button of his camera. In a tiny fragment of time, in one hundredth of a second, a flash of lightning interfered. In that hundredth of a second, its velocity had incredibly much time and space.
On the picture it reflects the meaning of its historical fragment, for lightning

as a weapon of God conceives and destroys at the same time, it is life and death. In a hundredth of a second the sides of time appeared, as well as the past, present and eternity, for the time spread into fire, which again and again destroys and fecundates the earth, as witnessed by the smaller photograph.

Our so diverse country as far as its landscapes are concerned is distinguished by some very different natural phenomena, the consequence of which are various natural disasters. Some greater catastrophes with numerous human victims are luckily unknown to us, but we certainly are badly affected by a number of rigours of the weather, such as (too) abundant rains or droughts. The experts comfort us that in our country we have no longer the disasters as known in the past. The reason for our conviction that there are increasingly more natural disasters they see in our ever greater sensitivity and vulnerability.

Earthquakes, floods, landslides, hails, frosts, droughts, destructive storms and sleet must be therefore accepted as fate which must, of course, bear it all, the evil and the good. We are least worried about floods, except in some valleys and in places along torrents. Where the earth is flat, however, such as in fields with slight inclination or in karst poljes (on the right is Lake Cerknica or, to be more precise, Cerknica polje), it takes into its palms some atmospheric water, until it kindly quenches its thirst, for example at Sorško polje (smaller photograph below). The upper smaller pictures denote how well the fields in the Pivka depression are soaked.

Water rolls, foams, swirls, flows, trickles, drips, bubbles, pounces, pours, inundates, brims over; water drips, rustles, murmurs, roars, gargles, sprinkles, absorbs, oozes, boils, streams, spits, runs dry, saps, swallows, leaks, flows away, flows into, melts, drowns, dissolves, sinks, freezes, decomposes, washes, enriches, supplies, surges, billows, lies, falls, fills, empties, rises, quenches one's thirst, escapes... how many verbs from its physics! And how many nouns from its chemistry: rain, shower, snow, frost, rime, glacier, slush, mud, pool, puddle, pond, stream, brook, river, lake, swamp, marsh, morass, fen, waterfall, geyser, sea, avalanche, backwater, rainwater, well, fountain... And how many meanings from its metaphysics: that it is the source of life, the power of purification, the condition of revival, the basis of creation... that it is the deeply planted and inaudible heart of our country reviving our veins with the loyalty of its pureness, wisdom and grace. It can be indifferent or faceless, free or caught in a litre. It can be blessed or abused, an exceptional natural tradition of our forefathers or a dirty companion to the ensuing generations; a creator or a destroyer, a spring or a torrent, an oasis or a whirlpool, alive or dead, fragrant or stinking, healthy or ill, peaceful or restless. Its is a place of revelation or a place of destruction. Water has a vernal, bright, deep, dormant, dead, sweet, sour, bitter, deliberate, enamoured, aggressive, emaciated face, as if a human being, as if having consciousness and subconsciousness. It is pregnant and sterile, eternally young and eternally old. Persistently and fugaciously it lives in our hearts and imagination, it is our need and our anguish. It is our fate, from the very creation, when the biblical spirit roamed above waters looking for a word. It is a very popular word in our language, its joy. Slovenia is very generous but also careless with water, and a country that simply cannot do without it.

When remembrance of Ice Age returns
to Bohinj, this deepest sinkhole in
the Slovene part of the Alps, we note
how those dark water birds, the white-
billed coots (the upper small
photograph) begin to disturb the winter
so much that it cannot fully fetter
the life on the lake. These joyous and
amusing birds have brought some
Mediterranean taste for community,
croaking, quarrelsomeness, playfulness
and, generally speaking, joy of living
into this grey and cold world. Upon
the icy plates they carry snow-white
coins of sun on their bills, they gleam
with them below the ice, hypocritically
offering them to the small fish.
And the sun, gratefully, is strewing
silver particles upon the lake and
the snowy cliffs above them.

On previous pages: *Here and there
the sun descends on Lake Bohinj from
the thickset clouds without totally
liberated from their yarn. In the lake's
mirror it looks at its pale unborn face.
At that time it becomes clear that this
naturally confined place has high
horizons, although it draws no natural
or temporal boundaries for the human
feelings.*

During the winter, watercourses lose some of their strength and speed. They are seemingly placid, and only occasional stormy puffs may carry away from them the cold fog, which eventually freezes on the banks of the Sava and Krka rivers (left and above). In the bed of the Bohinj Mostnica (right), enormous energy begins to accumulate at the end of the winter. The water sneakingly roars through the murky, devilish air ducts, bringing vernal news of the solar mysteries of the Triglav Mountains. In a minute or so it will foam in its solution cups, basins and hollows and with a guffaw swallow the icy column, which will no longer be able to melt in the rock.

During high waters they are mighty, during droughts they barely trickle or even dry up, in winter they halt in the icy columns, which are so hard that only climbers can clamber up them, like squirrels upon trunks. The waterfalls are constantly changing and rejuvenating, not only during the four seasons but also in the earth's life, which in comparison with man's seems timeless. As if somebody emptied, at the same time, thousands of huge barrels whose waters are, each in its own way, surprised and foaming because they suddenly lost ground. The waterfalls keep falling, constantly renewing their jets and drops, their currents of power and beauty attired in frills of the twinkling rainbows. They all have their own exciting life, depending on their water supply, shape of the ground and hardness of the rocks over which they fall. The softer the rock, the smaller they get. Slovenia boasts some 260 waterfalls. Some of them are very old, but they still behave as some eternal youngsters, such as the Savica (smaller photograph on the left below), which could be called the mother of Slovene waters. From Prešeren's epic poem The Savica Baptism onwards this waterfall has been felt as a spiritual source of the nation. After heavy rainfalls, the Triglav waters burst from their underground lakes under the mighty pressure and spill over the precipitous rockwalls of Mt. Komarča (left above and right below). The Boka near Bovec (smaller right photograph above), the highest Slovene waterfall comes roaring from the abdomen of some high mountains. In spring, a thousand tons of water falls some 106 metres deep per second. The Peričnik (larger photograph) has two waterfalls—16 and 52 metres high—and is an evident picture of a watercourse that has lost ground after the devastation left in the Vrata valley by the last glacier.

The Soča, ranked for its beauty amongst the first five Alpine rivers, initially flows through some tightly arranged mountains. It is enclosed by tall rockwalls leaning over it or standing slightly away from it, and from its tall narrow bed it keeps sending us freshness and chill, so benevolent in the summer heat. The water is hopping over the broken crags, and trickling from the side, across the patches of moss. Increasingly, the sounds of its parent stream are heard, the sounds of the rolling, whispering, thundering, roaring river. We also see its twinkling green and sky blue lights, as well as silver and gold colours bestowed on in by the sun. Everywhere we can see the wrinkling eyes of this witness of history, linking the two countries and two nations. The provocative mountains' daughter is leaping and hopping with such grace that one hides from her, in his excited heart, his instantly reduced ego. "But when you reach the plain, why this sudden calm?" addressed the Soča river the poet Simon Gregorčič buried along the church above the river. "You find it hard to part from hills, the cradle of your greeny waves?"

It is waters that gave the Slovene landscape its very unique character. Their drop through the limestone Dolenjska region is rather small, which is the reason why they do not load much gravel and sand. Instead of taking limestone away, the Krka and the Kolpa (smaller photograph above), even load it, dissolved, of course. Namely, the limestone brought into both rivers with hard water from numerous karst springs is freed by chemical processes on underwater plants. Mosses and algae die away in its stone "armour". The light and porous calcareous tufa thus grows on them, due to which the two karst rivers acquired their light brown and poriferous floor. During the summer, the rustling water is mostly low and tame; in fair weather it is pleasantly exposed to the sun and fairly warm.

If you were a gull, where above the Slovene coast would you choose to go? To the high flysch cliffs of Strunjan (smaller photograph below)? To the rocks below them, so rich with the little sea snails when the low tide takes away the waves? Above the Bay of Piran and its two prongs, for the first time in its history separated by the boundary (upper photograph)? Which wind would be the best for a loop above Piran (larger photograph)? The northwesterly? The easterly? Or perhaps the northeasterly called bora? Be careful! It could blow you away to the statue of the brilliant composer Tartini. In that case you should fiddle the Devil's Trill written for wind, violin and gull. In the end, the devil would even take you away. Allegro vivace! Hold out at least until largo. At that time the southeasterly wind would perhaps show mercy to you. With widely open mouth it would breathe the Sahara wind into the Piran Harbour, this most splendid town sitting room on our coast. Calmed and satisfied we could turn back into human, into being which has to be satisfied with the worm's eye-view. As far as gull is concerned, you would be left only with the freedom instinct, with con brio shaved by the wind.

Our beautiful Slovene language is
certainly secretly in love with the
Adriatic Sea (Jadransko morje),
for to the seafarers it bestowed, for
their age-old delight of travelling on
the Adriatic, the words jadro (sail),
jadranje (sailing) and jadrnica (sailing
boat). Sailors, the children of this sea,
no longer sail for the needs of survival,
but merely due to their loyalty to
the waves and wind, which is passion,
a mixture of love and hate, a challenge
of feelings between love and death, for
the sail is a symbol of the human heart,
in which passions dwell. The sailing
boat is, as claimed by some seafarers,
the bed of passions, which are

unsinkable. The Adriatic sailors love to
test the rose of winds in the Gulf of
Trieste, on their own or at regattas,
particularly around the Piran Punta,
where divers have their own
underwater Triglav, as the sea is
rather deep there—37 metres—enough
for a quick dive, and enough for a
couple of dolphins to imitate, as
people's friends, for example these two
excited girls, their consort.

When the sun is setting above Izola or Bernardin, it sometimes shows itself as a cruel illusion. It pokes into our hidden wishes for eternity, and this in the country which affords only 47 kilometres of coast. Along it there lie, tightly side by side, beaches, salt-pans, lagoons, roads, river mouths, industry, ports, warehouses, piers, towns, hotels, nature reserves, steep flysch walls, crags, brackish pools and marshes, inlets, mudflats... We are seriously thinking of building an artificial island near the coast, which should indeed be no problem for the Slovene engineers, considering that a third of our sea does not exceed 15 metres in depth. Thus we would get an artificial paradise, although in the midst of 400,000 people who live along the Gulf of Trieste, each of them using some 300 litres water per day. Can you imagine what has to be swallowed by our sea, which in contrast to politics knows no

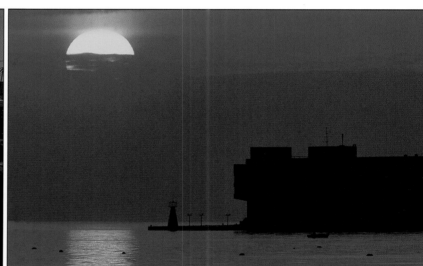

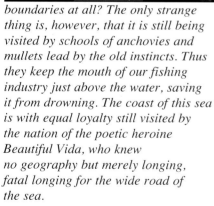

boundaries at all? The only strange thing is, however, that it is still being visited by schools of anchovies and mullets lead by the old instincts. Thus they keep the mouth of our fishing industry just above the water, saving it from drowning. The coast of this sea is with equal loyalty still visited by the nation of the poetic heroine Beautiful Vida, who knew no geography but merely longing, fatal longing for the wide road of the sea.

In the place where the bordering Dragonja spreads on its alluvia in a wide delta, salt-pans were built already by the ancient Romans. The system of shallow basins, crisscrossed with quays, channels, gates and levees, was on its 650 hectares strengthened particularly during the Austro-Hungarian empire, when the state kept for itself the monopolistic production of salt. At Lera (below) the salters still reap some five thousand tons of salt per year. In the greater part of the historical salt-pans, at the neighbouring Fontanigge (larger photograph), spreads a fantastic landscape of oblivion and decay.

The wise economic and ecological salt-pans system, on which the town of Piran was able to grow, has been run over by time. Nature, the loyal squire of time, began to turn the pans into a treasury of the plant and animal life. Fontanigge turned into the Mediterranean northernmost station for the migrating birds. More than 200 species rest and feed in the Fontanigge reeds and saltmarshes, while some 80 species actually breed there. A winged paradise! Which, however, may sink as early as in a hundred years, if our planet continues to warm up.

On previous pages: *Sea gate to the Piran Harbour, part of our splendid heritage of the Adriatic maritime culture*

So quiet and slow that one could count its ribs at the bottom, flows the Krka river along its picturesque canyon bed. In its upper course its pensiveness is disturbed particularly in places where fed by its numerous underground waters. Across the steps of calcareous tufa and artificial dams it flows in limpid rapids, most pleased to be able to show its unleashed power.
In the mid-twentieth century this almost 100 kilometres long karst river still powered 71 watermills and sawmills. Now it powers adrenalin in canoeists and kayakers, as well as in anglers each year after April 1st.

"*Don't carry my days, oh Mura, away from my view, but instead do please turn another pebble or two,*" sings Vlado Kreslin who brought some Pannonian feeling into Slovene music, the same as the dark and deep Mura brought into our waters, with its course across Slovene territory, much Pannonian peacefulness, the veiled beauty of Prekmurje and the rich world of its riverine woodlands and backwaters. Each year the strengtheners of its banks make sure that the river swollen with melted snow in its Alpine course does not look for new beds at Ravensko and Dolinsko. With its average slope

of 0.5°, the Prekmurje is the flattest region in Slovenia and its largest plain at the same time. The streams flowing across it into the Mura are again and again looking for their outlets, turning pebbles and stones and in doing so losing, in the soil, three quarters of their water–which is most pleasing to the farmers–creating numerous meanders as if trying to imitate man's path through life, as if they themselves would wish to grant Vlado's request, if the Mura cannot hear him well.

The emerald necklace of the seven Triglav lakes, situated in some 8 kilometres long and by glaciers hollowed valley of the upland karst (larger photograph), is the world of solitude, which smiles only in the sun. In the midst of high mountain ridges, rock beds and shelves, the Triglav waters are looking for and chiselling underground veins. In places where limestone beds are watertight or where basins are filled with gravel, they form tiny lakes. With greenish blue eyes they are turning back to the mountains, as if knowing that they flow on and that from their dark labour beds they will soon roar away with the mighty Savica waterfall. Nature is also deeply serious but somewhat narcissistic at Sleme (smaller upper photograph), below the wrinkled precipices of Travnik, Šit and Jalovec, which are looking at themselves in a sinkhole pond in the middle of a pasture. No wonder these peaks have fallen in love with themselves, for mountaineers simply adore them. And who is looking at itself in the tiny Lakes of Lovrenc on Mt. Pohorje (middle photograph) – Only the sky who perhaps sees in them the Laker, the shaggy being with long reddish-brown moustache, the merman who is always hungry of young female flesh. On the other hand it is quite possible that this upland marsh has already punished him, for the blue eyes of the Pohorje lakes are calm. So clam that they don't even give a wink to the sky. Similarly stiffens, here and there, the little Lake Jasna in the Pišnica valley near Kranjska Gora, the obedient mirror of Razor and Prisojnik, the mountain giants in the background.

The Sava, the highly strange river.
There is no watercourse that the
Slovenes would no better than this one,
for hundreds kilometres of railways and
road run along it. There is no river
than would be bridged more often than
this one. About its beauty, however,
about its enraptured meaning for
the health of Slovene waters they know
very little indeed; or, to be more
precise, they pay no heed to it. Namely,
the Sava is a maid of the Slovene
development, since in no less than
24 hours it washes away the greater
part of our filth. The Sava is also an
eternally tired housewife clearing up
after the indolent family, although its
used to being patient and to bear it all.
When putting on the attire of a large
river in the Posavje basin, you can at
times read a story about its sources,
about Savica and Zelenci, Rinka and
Kamniška Bistrica. Like mother she
hides, in her soul, the memory
of the bright moments of her children,
for example of the fairy river with no
less than seven names (Trbuhovica,
Obrh, Stržen, Rak, Pivka, Unica,
Ljubljanica), of her swallets, of her
waters spilled over fields and its
roaming around the Karst world, which
has more holes than Swiss cheese.
No wonder that as early as in the
Middle Ages Ljubljanica river
fascinated, with its mild terrestrialness,
clearness and secluded riverine
woodlands in the shelter of hills,
the Carthusians who near its boils at
Bistra (smaller middle photograph)
built their monastery. In it, the Slovene
Technical Museum is now developing
very well indeed, also at the expense
of the mighty technology and industry,
which enslaved the Sava waters.
The currents of history move in
mysterious ways.

On previous pages: *The islet in
the middle of lake Bled, celebrated as
Carniola's heavenly attire, is an
ancient cultic centre, which has
for millennia attracted people with
the grace of its place in time and space.
The authors of the guide through
the Mediterranean Europe from
the well-known series The Lonely
Planet have ranked Bled amongst
the ten most beautiful places in this
part of Europe.*

Has there ever been a lake in the Ljubljana Marshes? Or have the marshes been flooded for longer periods of time, as it may be seen on the larger photograph? These questions cannot be accurately answered even by science, let alone by the marshes' inhabitants or visitors excited by the original natural environment, which has already reached the southern suburbs of Ljubljana. In the channels and passages, by which the marshes were actually drained, water rises only after protracted rains. The caves left by peat diggers and archaeologists, bear witness to the former larger bodies of water, on which travelled, in their dugouts, the so-called lake dwellers of unknown Bronze Age people. The dreams of the drainers who wished to turn these wetlands into Ljubljana granary, did not come true, the same as many other plans according to which this extensive plain, often entangled in a more or less foggy atmosphere, was to become a profitable business entity. By a lucky chance, such materialistic illusion was not realised not even at the intermittent Cerknica polje (smaller photographs), which was very seriously planned to be turned into a permanent lake. But–can you make a dish out of a sieve? It is true that the largest Slovene lake spills over here and there in this area–even in no more than three days after heavy downpours. But the same caves, which like from sunken nipples of nature spew up water, begin to suck this same water back again in a few weeks and send it, along the underground water courses, towards the Ljubljana Marshes. And further on: not only towards the Sava and the Black Sea, but also – through evaporation–into the air and clouds, into the eternal circle in which water lives.

On previous pages: *After the heavy autumn rains, lake Cerknica rises so high and so suddenly that in the traditional orchards of the village of Dolenje Jezero it lifts the apples that have fallen not far away from their trees. At the end of its life, the wretched unpicked fruit turned into a fugacious adornment of the melancholic countryside. Soon it will fertilise the floating material of the waters which – like in the sun above – are writing their mysterious stories in the earth below.*

The Krka river at Krško polje (larger photograph below), the lake Bohinj (larger and smaller photographs above), and a lake at Cerknica (smaller photograph below) under the flaming sun. It is quietly drowning in it and exiting it through some other door. The sun, on the other hand, is making wonders, changed and enriched with the water's numerous powers. It is changing forms, creating them anew, it is rising high, then falling down again–always turned towards its crystal portrait. The latter remains constant and numb, although full of reveries passed on by the sun. Water is a soft, eternally travelling being. It multiplies dreams about something to be, about something the sun is losing.

On next pages: *Thunderclouds, as part of the eternal circling of water, above Kosovel's pines near Tomaj in the Karst, "wearily whispering in silent dismay…"*

If water is the mother, then wood is her son, a truly strapping fellow. Which is the best presented in the legend about Christopher, the giant who carried the child of God over a stream, the child as heavy as the world. In thanks for his strength and loyalty, his ferryman's stick grew green.

The Slovene people, on the other hand, began to believe that a look at Christopher's icon on a church's outer wall protected them from unexpected death. In the second folk tradition, wood is again a symbol of resuscitation, such as the wooden mask of the Runner from the area of Cerklje or as the Green George. It is a material used for home or cosy family life, as witnessed by the following Carinthian carpenter song: "Hey, lass, you better take me, for I'm a carpenter and I'll make a cottage for thee, as well as a cradle and child, you will see ..." This was the Carinthian Adam who tried to make, for Eve, a surrogate Eden out of wood. And even wood is, in a way, a material that was exiled from Eden. Wood is a Slovene word for forest, while forest is a true Eden, for it is the highest form of plant communities. It retains the balance of processes in the soil and is capable of sucking, with deep roots, dead matter from great depths. It is capable of making humus and living soil, it is retaining memory of our forefathers who were the forest people. It awakens and strengthens the thought that with its necessity and extent it is fatal for the Slovene community, for it shapes and feeds it. Time cuts into wood its signs, while man shapes it with masterly strokes of his knowledge. Trees are not used merely for logs, and logs are not used merely for boards and firewood. A forest can be a store of freshness, water and warmth, the source of new life, a refuge or a sanctuary where man's heart can grow green just as Christopher's dry stick.

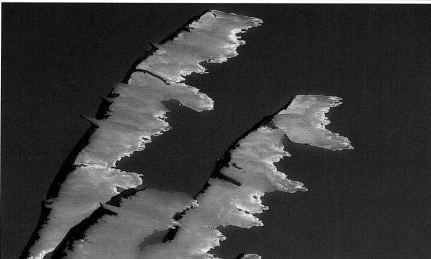

The glittering winter wind is
uncovering the light of melting sleet on
tree branches and snowdrifts' peaks,
the light of transitory forms, the thicket
of icy sails and silvery reefs that have
clung to trees and beams. To
a traveller it uncovers the fugacious
solitude and the vital force of wood,
either dead or succulently alive and
supple. Towards the peaks of the sky
it stretches the pleading hands of larch
trees, it stretches them with a command
for a different deliverance: let this sun
climb finally higher in the sky, let
it bring some pure morning serenity.

A not particularly bright person is called "beechen" according to the Slovene folk tradition. This is of course unjust – unjust for the beech, which is certainly a wise tree. It sensibly regulates its life, especially during its winter repose. This is why it is the most widespread tree in our forests. Even as early as during the first heavy frost it gets rid of its leaves and thus protects itself from the loss of nutrients. The thick layer of the fallen off leaves protects soil organisms from the bitter winter cold. However, when the leaves decompose, they become a true feast for the roots. Beech trees are also able to wisely withstand any competition, to be very patient in the shade, which gives them the decisive advantage in the struggle for their place under the sun with other light-loving trees. This is why they rejuvenate well. The skills in handling with them are old; they are passed down from generation to generation, like in Bohinj (smaller photograph below), where they say that lumberjacks must have long legs due to being forced to transport beech in deep snows.

The roundish ridges and the chilly basins of the Pokljuka plateau are covered mainly with spruce forests, which suits the sharp Alpine climate in the area more than 1,000 metres above sea level, with the average annual temperature of 3° C and abundant precipitation, half of it in the form of snow. The slim and tall Pokljuka beauties, the most precious among them being the so-called "resonant spruce", which is suitable for the manufacture of musical instruments, are a true pride of the Slovene forestry. Pokljuka attained its first management plan as early as in 1837. Pokljuka forests are ranked amongst the most

beautiful in Europe. There are no clearings on the plateau. In contrast to the colleagues on the other side of the Karavanke (seen together with the Savinja Alps in the background of the larger photograph), our foresters do not cut them bare but merely thin the stands in order for the young trees to obtain more sun for their growth. This is why from the Pokljuka mountains the dark undulating forests are seen as a sea pleasantly smelling of ozone and resin. And this scent does not disappear even in cottages (smaller photograph above) built on Pokljuka from the neighbouring wood.

Wood preserves, until the very end, its remembrance of the sun with which it breathed while still growing in a forest. The small boards, combined into an ornamental nucleus of rustic door by a master joiner, can be compared with the low tide on the coast. From it retracted the high tide of the sun's live radiation, but the memory of the sun remains, the memory of the treasure called photosynthesis, on which actually depends our world, from which the costs of our life must also be paid . This is the memory which is longer than life. It is a dry flower of the sun, a circle of life from greenery to rainbow.

*The lime tree God at Ptujsko polje
and the ladder on the charcoal-burning
pile in the Dolenjska region show
themselves as two landmarks of life,
i.e. height and depth. The first is a high
secluded wood on the coast of air with
the halo of God's warm breath. It is lit
up by purple evening, with the glitter
of the sun, which can no longer be
seen. It became deaf to the hours,
which cut time into fragments, it is
blind to the light and the seasons. It is
full of silence, in which voices that are
trying to nullify it are heard. It is silent
as in front of Pontius Pilate, due to
which we often wonder whether if it at
all is. Well, the truth is that this is how
we also deal with our heart when
having no heartache; as if we didn't
have one. And the ladder, does it mean
something more than an instrument
with which the charcoal man protects
himself from falling into the pile and
himself turning into charcoal?
Symbolically, it certainly means more
than that. Man is ladder. In himself
he rises to the sky and falls into hell.
While climbing, the ladder fills him
with fear and anxiety, and while
descending he is welled up by joy,
by the feeling of safety. Or vice versa.
For the fact is that humans are
somehow torn in themselves.*

In Istra and the Karst, the sycamine is a house tree. From its sweet fruits, the father makes brandy to quench his spiritual thirst, while the mother makes a thick syrup for the short winded kids to quench their body thirst in the summer. The gnarled and distorted sycamine, however, stays at the house like some old spouseless aunt in the midst of the haughty, slim Refosco vines, which nicely embraced on the trellises huddle against the family nest. It perseveres in its life, and every spring it allows to be trimmed to her master's taste, a docile enjoyer, again and again fettered in the concreted yard.; and thus it remains, from

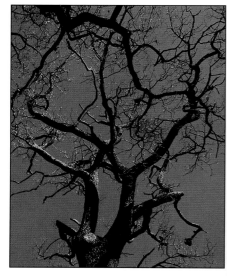

generation to generation, a silent mark of the homestead, becoming the tree of life. On the model of the oak tree (smaller photograph) it pumps this life from above, as its crown, when getting ready for new shoots, is similar to roots.

Wood in the shape of larch shingles on the roof; a wooden shepherd's dwelling at the montane pasture of Laz near Bohinj; a corner made of chestnut beams and a Bela krajina cottage – nothing but wood recording time and life in its annual rings. Wood as heritage, tradition of all generations living in the Alps, Dinaric Karst or on the Pannonian plains. Wood, in which messages of some old culture on Slovene soil have rotted, but then germinated, like in woods from putridity, new seeds on which we live today. Wood, which in its annual rings inscribes the rigours of the weather and the consequences of man's attitude towards forests. Such wood is constantly renewed, it is the omnipresent bridge between the past and future, it is the source of words and songs, belief and unbelief, safety and unsafety, warmth and cold, greed and modesty, happiness and seclusion. Wood is a friend sent to us by fate.

On previous pages: *Harmony of wood and the traditional residential culture in a Bela krajina home. The beams and the constantly embellished little windows speak of the mysteries of the distant past.*

The ancient rural master, Najevnik from Ludranski vrh in the Koroška region, believed that the good spirit of the Ludranski vrh community would live in the village lime tree. Some 700 years ago he thus planted a family of seven little limes, which soon began to grow in a common trunk. Eventually they grew into the thickest Slovene tree. Its circumference reached twelve metres, which is yet another fairy tale number. Still, what happened to the good spirit of the human community? Does it still live in the Najevska lime tree? Has it moved to under the roof of the ancient plague mark, which we can see in the background of the larger

photograph? Into the sign directing walkers or travellers on its wall to fill them with the feeling of safety? Has it lignified in the freshwater perch under the old jambs? Is it dying away under the roof shingles of the Solčava farm? Is it growing green on the wooden pyramids of the Bohinj barns, which imitate the spirit of the shape of "the grey chief of the Carniolan snow-covered mountains"?

is one was planted by a storm in
 barren land, the other by a farmer
 let his neighbours know how his tree
 a master to itself, the same as he is;
 third was procreated by a chance
racle of conception… Each of
 sixteen plants on our photographs
 its own story to tell in no more than
o words: solitary tree… Trees are
ns with which nature teaches
 lonesome people how to hold out
d suppress their wishes.

Uršlja gora, the worshipped mountain (smaller photograph below), is the great mother of the Koroška region, mighty even when sitting down. Mt. Peca (in the middle) is her bald sister, who is always calling on somebody but never wants to sit down. Smrekovec (larger photograph) is the last active volcano in Slovene territory. To the left from it is Sv. Križ above Bele Vode with two little pilgrimage churches and a fine view. Under the mossy ground, lively springs are flowing, but it is only here and there that they show their flashy mouths. At altitudes where forests most often end in the Alpine world, beech trees still strive on the border between the Koroška and Štajerska regions. While elsewhere the solitary trees are already defying the storms on barren land and stretching their dry knotty limbs, here the larches are spreading their crowns safely and with ease. Due to the fertile soil, warm westerly winds and a greater number of sunny days than in the valley, farmers had settled on the upland land. The inhabitants of the Koroška and Štajerska regions love to take a walk in the upland Garden of Eden, above their little big world washed by winds and the sun.

When its leaves display themselves,
before falling off, in some of its most
beautiful colours – yellow, sunburnt,
flaming, dying out – the beech tree is
airy, open although still shady, bare
and mysterious. Everywhere we can
smell the odour of highly fulfilled life.
How easy and gentle is the burial of
the leaves. The forest floor is reached
by the rustling dry brown rain, which
bounces off joyously if walked upon by
humans. It whirls with them, while
the trunks stand there solemnly, like
monuments of an ancient order in
nature. But the latter looks as if not
caring about the autumn beauty at all.
Wood has finished sucking its own

blood, its veins are pleasantly full.
It is sleepy with satiation. From its
richly spread table a lot of brown
breadcrumbs will still fall off,
so nutritious for all those beggarly
caterpillars, fungi, mosses, snails,
slugs, frogs, lizards, earthworms,
microbes and ticks, all those godly
beings which of course must live
as well.

It shakes in the northeasterly wind and sheds its seeds into the dry-stone walls. In the Karst commons it even manages, here and there, to squeeze itself between the rocks. Its leaves flicker like a swarm of butterfly wings, its flowers rise like a cluster of a thousand retractile snail horns, covered by the sun with nectar-like coating. Thus the wig tree's flowers try to sweeten the torments of its dry growth in this rather desolate soil. Thus it fills itself with the sun, turning into a large yearly sundial. It borrows all its colours, until it spreads, in the Karst, the altars of its lost blood. At that time it would like to be as precious and worshipped as the Teran wine, for in their stupefying red colours – ruby and bordeaux – they are in fact brothers. But only by nature, nor by their humanness. This is why the wig tree, when the prettiest, smiles less and less.

In fog, the larch trees are sometimes even more attractive than in the sun and wind. With their saggingly straightened branches they rise from the grey whiteness, from the rustling silence of the Alpine virgin forest. Suddenly it seems that they are sighing deeply, that they try to perfuse their vital juices once more, before shedding the golden needles. The neighbouring spruces seem too dark to them for a bearable symbiosis, the rocks on which they grow keep pinching them like too tight and with ice covered boots. Slender, lopped and badly whipped by mountain gales they are now sowing thousands of seeds, as if this is the only thing on which depended their survival in the destructive horrors of the mountain winter, which will soon close the door of earth with its snow bolts.

Is it possible that some forest goblin has been secretly visiting the studio of the Slovene painter France Mihelič? Is it possible that it was this goblin who has shaped, after Mihelič's demonic figures, this pile of trees somewhere along the tree line in the Julian Alps? Larch trees, distorted from the weight of snow on their shoulders, seem to be inhabited with the apparitions of demons of the montane country, they remind the people of their simultaneous world of poetry and horror. Just all of them have been knocked down by the flashes of lightning, punished for being so attracted to the silence of the sky. The trees invite all those wood eaters

and lichens, spiders and mosses to the feast behind the bark. Due to which now follows only the process of putrefaction and mouldering. But the forest goblin is already waiting patiently, by order of this fate, for the little beasts from the studio to satisfy their hunger, he is already trimming a cradle for a new germ, for a new bark.

Not only the Notranjska region as shown on our pictures (such as the Rebrnice below Mt. Nanos on the larger photograph), but almost half of Slovenia is covered by forests. There is almost no farmland without them: only on less than a fifth of the country's surface. Due to this incredible fact we have of course a tremendous number of forest edges (such as the one on the upper photograph), where grasslands and forests meet. The foresters have estimated that the forest edges in Slovenia, if put together, would encircle the Earth. Delicately inserted into this physically small country, they are a special

aesthetic value of its landscape. Ecologists would add that the forests are, on account of so numerous edges across the country, favourably arranged and that for this reason they radiate certain health; they are keeping the country vital, capable of renewing its natural sources. They catch more water and send it on well purified. They clear the atmosphere and are never sick, for they are protected by selfhealing. Our life therefore depends on the art of symbiosis with the forests and their constantly creative nature.

On previous pages: *A forest at Pivško podolje. Some of the trees are still green, others rusty with time.*

Snow blends all kinds of light, it lies
like a burden of the expired years,
sleeps here and there with the goddess
Morana. On it descends and from it
rises the tide of water vapours. Snow
mixes up all trees, it takes away
the shape of paths and fences, due to
which we no longer know the way and
their meaning. Gently it outlines, with
white colour, the tremendous efforts
of willow trees, to make them to grow
higher, through rotation, than destined
by man. Snow, this eternal child,
is placing cold flakes of cotton wool
on the wounds of the old tree mothers
to relieve their expectation of the
coming spring.

Stone is not just a small hard ball of densely packed minerals as usually described by dictionaries. It can also be a milestone, cornerstone, kidney stone, foundation stone, philosophers' stone, keystone, grindstone, flintstone, cobblestone, touchstone, etc. It could be the foundation of Christian ethics: "Let the man without sin throw the first stone," said Christ. Stone is closely associated with human speech, as well as with man's heart or even with his fate, e.g. "Water doesn't run under a lying stone", "Constant dripping hollows out a stone", "A rolling stone gathers no moss". Who amongst us have never found themselves "between the upper and the nether millstone"? The wretched innocent stone can also be the main protagonist in literature (for example in a short novel, shorter than a human breath: "Your heart is turning into stone." "The stone which beats for you," says she. And after five years she crushed his head with it.) At times it seems that stone is home to spirits which would otherwise haunt a human soul; as if spirits were lichens, beings constantly struggling for their survival. Stone stoically bears it all. It loves rain and snow, for these natural elements softens and thin it, as it is only in this way that it can get overgrown with seemingly motionless time. Stone is merely sand in a large hourglass, which is running out. Even the mountains, our great pyramids of stripped stone, are only a contact with time. Only a moment, when the waves of the earth have been here and there brought to a standstill.

The matter can be easily explained by the experts: water or ground moisture evaporates due to the warmed up air or solar radiation in the plains. Vapours are invisible. In the morning chill they gather in drops, in more or less thick veils, which float and sometimes rise very high. At the Bohinj montane pasture Krstenica (larger photograph), the veils reached the attitude of 1700 metres and began to disintegrate. A mountaineer wandered about the dark pathless country. The smaller photographs show two somewhat clearer scenes from Bohinj – the Studor mountain and kozolecs with hayricks below it and the belfry of St. John's church at Ribčev laz – and a view from above the Vrata valley at Mts. Rjavina and Triglav.

On previous pages: At dawn, "half of Slovenia", as we love to boast of our numerous views, can be seen from the Triglav Mountains. In the morning glow bathes the Gorenjska plain, with the peaks of the Karavanke and Savinja-Kamnik Alps rising in the background.

*A happy little child in the arms of
a round, soft motherly stone smiling
from afar in radiant colours in
the middle of gloomy rocky solitude.
It will never reach the proud height
of its larch lineage. Even after dying
it will not experience the protracted
death of a tree defying the heavy
mountain gales. It seems more like an
ephemeral butterfly, which decided
to be a little flower and had to pollinate
itself. During the storms this little larch
is meek, in rainy weather it is hungry,
while in the autumn it is thankful
to itself for losing the golden little
bunches of needles, with which it will
feed the meagre scree, its cradle. When*

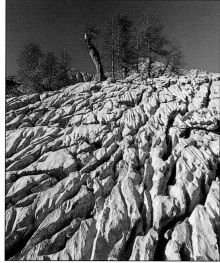

*snow-broth and rainwater flow freely
down the rocky surface, sullenly
wrinkled little channels are made
higgledy-piggledy in the limestone
substratum. When water is looking
for its own course, like over these
venerable 99 steps on Bled Islet,
it often gnaws through and shifts
the stone slabs.*

According to Janko Mlakar, the Slovene mountaineers can be divided into: common mountaineers (homo alpinus vulgaris) who can be found everywhere except in low country, mountain yodellers (homo alpinus ululans) who shout just everywhere and also love to yodel, especially on the peaks; mountain reptiles (homo alpinus reptans) who live only in uplands and even there only in rockwalls, preferably northern ones; mountain skiers (homo alpinus hiemalis) who have their feet strongly elongated in front and at the back and are therefore well qualified for sliding down the snow; and mountain fleas (homo alpinus pulex) who have steel spikes on their boots, which enable them to walk on ice. To this almost a century old biology of the special breeds of Slovenes, who make up approximately a tenth of the nation, we could add the so-called mass mountaineer, participant of numerous companies which in ant-like ranks besiege Mt. Triglav, or participant of memorial marches, for example to Porezen (the third of the smaller photographs). A special subspecies of the mountain yodeller is the bandsman who accompanies mass mountaineers. Homo alpinus, who is always looking for new challenges to the capacities of his body and mind, but is bringing to the mountains all his good and bad habits from the low country, is thus becoming homo alpinus multiplex.

The mountaineers moving downwards
from Mt. Špik to the Pišnica Valley
(larger photograph) are only fleeting
extras in the geological drama of
the Julian Alps and the Karavanke, as
also seen in the scenery of Podrta gora
in the garland of the Lower Bohinj
Mountains (upper smaller photograph)
or of Begunjščica in the Karavanke
(picture below). The western and
northern rocks, built along nothing but
vertical lines, are being washed by
the white light. The beautiful southern
clouds are ploughing the sky with
widely spread sails. Although
the mountaineers should be always
careful where to place their feet, their

gazes are constantly escaping to
the wide mountain landscape. Without
a break, their eyes are sliding to
the very precipices above the deep
valleys, while their beholders often
do not know whether the space is truly
experienced by them or whether
they are merely dreaming.

*When the sun's morning glow begins
to warm Mt. Triglav (larger
photograph), this royal mountain
becomes attired in royal crimson.
A looker-on is excited and appeased at
the same time, just as during his
primary happiness for watching fire.
The first to grow pale are the dark
purple colours. When the sun rises,
the red colours shudder for a few
moments, then shout… double… and
even treble. Soon a huge curtain
of rocks, ice and snow falls over this
colour spectacle and from then on
the sky is covered more faintly by it.
Behind this rock curtain we can see
the depths of the Slovene wide expanses
and the immense precipices below
Mt. Triglav. The mighty Triglav's
conical shadow, which can be seen on
the upper smaller photograph, reaches
very far, even as far as Ljubljana,
during the summer sunset. If the lit
Triglav is looked at from the evening
side, from the other side of the day's
golden spine, as pictured from Sovatna
(middle photograph), this patriarch
is even prouder for being the last one
in the country to look at itself in all its
glory, so manly unicorned. As if not
caring about its three heads (Triglav
meaning literally "three-headed").
If, however, our highest mountain
is watched from the southern
or southwestern side, as admiringly
viewed by the majority of Slovenes,
it stands in accordance with its name,
very high and alone (lower
picture showing a view of it from
Soriška planina).*

On previous pages: *Mt. Stol, the highest
peak in the Karavanke. Bled Castle
is an aristocratic nest, boldly built on
the precipitous wall high above Lake
Bled. Even more boldly and even
higher the mountain cottage as seen on
the right peak of Stol was built.
The cottage was given its name after
France Prešeren, the greatest Slovene
poet, who was born in the village
of Vrba below Stol.*

...me order in the confusion of
... Julian peaks is made by the valleys
... they follow each other on our
...otographs from left to right: Tamar,
...všica, Trenta and Vrata. This is
...unch of the four prettiest valleys in
... Julian Alps, the workshops of
...uds, the kind cradles of the Slovene
...untaineering. The sun is joyous,
...en strewing separate sheaves of rays
...rough the mist when judging what
...light and what is dark. On the cutting
...ges of the rockwalls, the thick mists
... mists show their flabby longevity,
...iting to be swallowed by the winds
...o their knotted bowels. And the
...nds as winds: the sun forces them
...ways anew to blow up
... the mountain peaks only utterly
...ansed. At times, however, they
...have hypocritically: in the shades
...y instil into a mountaineer
... feeling of danger, the feeling that
...y might soon bluster like storms
...ound his pounding heart.

The Klemenšek homestead (larger
photograph) above the Logarska
Valley at an altitude of 1145 metres,
on a sunward terrace under Mt.
Olševa, reflects a self-confident rural
remoteness from the valley, a very
special view on the world, the fireside
warmth from the distant past.
Who knows in which century the first
Klemenšek settled on this soil, bold
and desperate enough to reclaim
the land–not for the sake of
the exceptional view of the Grintovci
mountains from Ojstrica to Mrzla gora
(as seen in the background), but for
the sake of survival. His neighbours
living on similar sunward terraces
under Olševa–the Macesniks, Rogars,
Potočniks, Ošovniks, Prodniks and
Robniks–fought the same battles in
the steep haymeadows, pastures and
woodlands, looked after self-sufficiency
of their husbandry as well as for
the family order and simple culture, so
very necessary for their survival during
the long winters. In the springtime the
beauty takes a breather, gets rid of
the winter patches and takes a walk,
completely white and rested, across
the meadows, as if setting out on
a merry wedding feast with the sun.
In the glacier valleys, at Roban's
Corner (upper smaller picture) and
Koritnica (lower photograph),

everything is blooming in the festive
colour of the awoken earth in the open
country of the torrential alluvial
deposits and in the dark cradles of
the meditative forests.

In the Karst, sunlit stones can be seen at every step, in numerous forms. On them, the step slackens and the strong northeasterly bora feels just like at home. The Karst people have been for millennia cutting limestone for their fireplaces, consoles, steps, well-heads, tombstones, chimneys, window frames, keystones, gutters, portals, walls, roofs… Of the Karst stonecutter they used to say: "There is no stone he couldn't break, and no barrel he couldn't empty." His life actually remained in stone, and his soul is seen as an apparition in this greyly stripped, rough and solid matter, rejuvenated always anew.

As a square monolith or as a slab, stone can be a sign of memory of somebody, as at the Podnanos cemetery (smaller photograph above). It can also be the elementary material for a town or its walls (as at Vipavski Križ on the photograph below). It can be a material for the oldest art, sculpture, which on the very account of stone became the most material art, but at the same time art which most directly transforms matter into spirit. (The middle picture from a Roman tombstone made of Pohorje marble shows a fight in the antique arena.) On the larger photograph we see flysch stone cut into window and door frames and blocks for dry-stone walls at an abandoned house in the Istran village of Abitanti. And as far as the two cautious, grumbling hens on the photographs are concerned, we, the Slovenes, have the following saying: "Even a blind hen can find a grain." Their henhouse has become the house, which will not crumble into ruins for a long time, as the stone piled up without mortar will persevere for ages as an evidence that folk housebuilders knew the basics of its physics. Stone has always been at their hand and good for everything, for a place of the alive or for the place of the dead, for the portraits of life-and-death struggles and, in the end, of mere lingering on.

Stone by stone, and it still holds water.
Have a look at the gutters on the upper
stone well-head on the larger
photograph or on the smaller picture
below. Each of them has enough space
to be, in its own way, deep and distinct.
They were shaped by the people who
chose purely by instantaneous
inspiration as to where they shall drop
or raise buckets on ropes. In these
gutters some Karst Mediterranean ease
is reflected. A well in the Karst yard
still holds water. Its depth is silence.
If you want to have a look at it,
it moves like mystery. The echoing
human voice ages instantly, it sinks into
itself in the stone-walled cylinder.
The source of life is deep.
In the narrow circle, in the precipitous
distance you can see no end to its
loyalty and darkness. The well of
the Karst tradition is deep,
seemingly bottomless.

Let it be the saint standing on a console in the wall of the Karst church, the cross with the image of Christ from Gora at Trnovski gozd, Peter's wayside cross from Vrhpolje in the Vipava Valley, or the five metres high statue of Orpheus standing in the centre of Ptuj as the highest Roman monument chiselled out of a single block of stone in Central Europe–each of these statues and crosses was originally just a shapeless block of stone. It is hard to believe although absolutely natural that a stone dressed with the hand of a master, full of love, turned into a surge of spirit, into an infinite shivering of tiniest vibrations, into

a play of almost unnoticeable details, which testify that the stone surface submits itself to the laws of the stone's silent core.

Otlica is hollow. It is a natural window, looking like a huge drop, in the very edge of the Trnovska plateau. This hole, through which diabolical gusts of wind can be often heard, used to come in very handy to the people of Vipava and the Highlanders when visiting each other, trading, getting married or engaged in other human activities. Geologists have explained its origin with a large crack that had formed at the junction of the two huge fault blocks. Water finally broke through the wall, which has till today widened into some 20 metres high and 15 metres wide window. In the duel of the folding layers the second half is now to follow,

another millions of years, which is quite inconceivable for the human perception of time, even for our historical feeling. And it is this feeling by which we can measure the rise and decline of two places: the town of Ajdovščina below Otlica (smaller photograph below) and the Istran village of Osp (above). The old town is still squeezed between the partially preserved Roman town walls, while the Istran village has boldly settled at the foot of the collapsed rockwalls on the edge of the Karst plateau.

The passages of the Postojna and Škocjan Caves (smaller photograph below), the two greatest natural treasures of the Slovene Karst, are high and wide, and in places they even expanded into actual chambers with the never changing temperature of 8.2° C. The calcite system is few thousand years old and still growing: for a millimetre in a decade. Its is extremely rich, mainly due to the abundant rainwater trickling through the cave ceilings. At the same time it is also extremely diverse as far as its colours and shapes are concerned, for it has just everything, from miniatures to giants, such as

the stalactite actually called "The Giant", which with its 16 metres in height consists of some 1,400 cubic metres of calcite. The hanging, standing and wall dripstones (in the shape of curtains, baldachins and covers) are often coupled in columns and stone waterfalls. Predjama Castle, which also reminds us of some bizarre scenographic conception, seems as if growing out of stone, as if sewn to 123 metres high wall. The narrow residential part of the Castle continues with Karst passages branched out in a couple of storeys, linked with a series of abysses. It reflects the spirit of brave and inventive noblemen.

From Mt. Triglav, Slovenia looks like a rough sea which, however, was in a distant moment brought to a standstill. The larger photograph depicts a view of Kanjavec and Krn, while on the smaller picture a view of Škrlatica can be seen. From Triglav we cannot see, however, the thick network of long and interwoven mountain paths, not even the longest and probably the most beautiful Slovene path, the famous Alpine transversal, which rises, descend or gently undulates from Maribor to the sea in the Gulf of Trieste. Is it at all possible to estimate the distances of its most demanding sections, such as across the long

stretches of scree, through draught-holes in northern walls and across rocks jagged with pitons? The length of the central mountain path can be best assessed on the basis of the time needed to traverse it. The sum is no less than 230 hours. And if a quickfooted trekker covers four kilometres per hour, we get respectful 920 kilometres, more, for example, than if making a pilgrimage to Rome. And this up hill and down dale, in scorching heat and fog, thirsty and tired, but, after all, happy. Due to this industriousness and willingness we, the Slovenes, have incurred more than 7,000 kilometres of mountain paths.

On the left is the solitary Vrh nad Peski in the Tolmin mountains, still dreadfully marked with the memory of World War I, while on the right we can see Hudi Vršič in the Kanin mountains, a piece of art by nature, composed of the mighty beds of karst limestone. Skiers love to descend to the giant kneading table of Tiha dolina below Kanin, feeling the safe nearness of the upper station of the Kanin cable railway. In the middle run two quite safe, mostly level and with pleasant paths interwoven glacier valleys, crown princesses of mass tourism in the upper Soča valley, the Trenta with Lepo Špičje in the background (above) and Loška Koritnica below Mangart and Jalovec (below).

Baron Karel Zois (1756–1799), the renowned Slovene botanist, was indeed free to say that the Valley of the Triglav Lakes was a "detestable stone desert", but he had such vein of natural science that he himself financed the first mountain cottage to be built in this very valley, not only to the glory of mountaineering but also to botany, which was in the 18th century a particularly honoured scientific study. In a rift he found the most beautiful endemic Slovene Alpine plant of the of the genus of bell-shaped flowers, eventually named after him as Zois' bellflower Campanula zoysii (larger photograph). However, this pale blue, narrow, tubelike and at its mouth hairy flower is not the only charming beauty of the Julian summer flora. From the light balconies, from rubble, from the barely perceptible talus we can see hundreds of the Triglav mountains flower species are smiling at us, of which let us present on this occasion the following eight (from left to right): yellow mountain saxifrage, buttercup, hairy alpenrose, mountain chives, gentian, alpine toadflax, edelweiss, chickweed.

The mythological stone apparitions, such as Krn (smaller photograph), Široka peč and Špik in the Martuljek group (larger photograph), make an impression even on somebody who loves mountains only from below. The dangers of cliffs and dark deeply incised ravines, falling steeply from the jags of the ridges and hiding numerous graves of the Slovene mountain climbers and the wretched soldiers from World War I, seem like a postcard from the safe distance of montane pastures. The wide and nicely vaulted head of Krn and its thickset, wrinkled body inspired the poetic world of Simon Gregorčič, who as a child tended sheep at the foot of this mountain. He yearned for it all his life, as for some paradise lost, of which speaks his famous verse "Back on this heavenly track." The Slovene Alpine dairy culture, which probably originates from the Celts, is in some aspects, such as summer grazing and curdling on montane pastures, still alive.

*The same as Zeus carried off, in
the form of a bull, the naive Phoenician
princess Europa and raped her–as
depicted on the smaller photograph
from the marble relief on the Roman
tombstone in the Šempeter
necropolis–the demon of war
kidnapped and raped the continent
of Europe in the middle of its carefree
and joyous period in the early 20th
century. In the Soča basin, one of
the most dreadful fronts in the first
World War kept raging for no less than
three years. During the senseless
massacre, as well as of the rigours
of the weather and illnesses almost
a million people died on the Soča front.
More than 7,000 Italians lie in the
monumental ossuary along the Church
of St. Anthony above Kobarid. Behind
the ossuary stands the despondent,
unfriendly Polovnik mountain, which
is still strewn, like other Soča
battlegrounds, with rusty iron,
grotesquely criss-crossed with tunnels,
caverns, wires and crevices in which
the mouldered human bones have
further strengthened the soil's fertility.
The place is full of military paths,
which no longer lead anywhere except,
perhaps, to the thought of the absurdity
of it all. But the shady, deep Trenta on
the picture, equally affected during
the war, has retained some pleasant
memories: of the Trenta hunters and
mountain guides, the soft-hearted
people, as called by Julius Kugy.
When the storms abate and when
the thundery torrents rush away,
a tiny hoping human remains on
the sieve of nature.*

On the sunny side of the Alps–in the background of the photographs are the sunward sides of the Lower Bohinj Mountains–the life of the horses used to be nothing but drudgery. Today they are, seemingly untamed, galloping up and down the unmown meadows, as seen on this picture from Zgornja Davča. Horse is yet again becoming an aristocrat among domestic animals; a living sign of youthful fieriness and desire. Its symbolic connection with natural forces and the four basic elements – earth, water, air and fire – has never ceased. The number of those who would like to mount it is rising again, as written by our poet Kocbek:

"Our horses came galloping from afar and are intended to go far, while the engines like to stall… and our path is long, too long to cover it on foot."

On previous pages: Zajamniki montane pasture above Bohinj, known also as "Triglav Street", and the thickset mountains in the background, all smelling of cheese: Debeli vrh, Škednjovec, Kanjavec, Mišelj vrh and Tošc (behind which rises who else but Father Triglav).

The prominent old tree still defying the mountain gales above Velo polje (left) along the path leading from Pokljuka to Triglav. This is its memorial photograph. Now it is merel a coppice. It fought clouds and stones this mountain angel. Secluded in its struggle, but alive in the memory of thousands of mountaineers as a victim it went through centuries, winged but armless and eyeless, a fragment of life in the almost everlasting stones.
On the right we see a cross on Mt. Viševnik above Pokljuka. It is not a sepulchral cross and not just a symbol of Christ, it is simply an upland announcement made of larch. It speaks of the separation of the four elements and their characteristics, so distinct in the upland world: the hot, the dry, the moist, and the cold. The socle fixed in the ground delineates faith in primary nature, persistence. The upper prong, rising towards the sky, delineates hope, its width signifying friendship. At the top of Viševnik, the cross also symbolises Mt. Triglav, on which our gaze stops after scanning the entire mountain chain. The destormed poetry of our highest mountain floats above its subjected landscape, and the Triglav white walls rise like a paragon of beauty for the Gorenjska country.

During the sunset, the Julian mountains virtually glow, as if the sun has just forged a number of huge sword blades. Look how from one of them, Mt. Špik in the Martuljek group (on larger photograph), the mighty walls are falling steeply – or rising from the wild precipices. And there are columns and crests undulating on other photographs, or jags and bold prongs piercing the horizon. Snowslopes are sliding the dark tongues into the ravines and crevasses, folding in scree and on mountain pines, in deep solitude. The omnipresent stones, the heritage of glaciers, which hid some of their remains under the flayed skin of the earth, the omnipresent golden, friendly relations before dusk, which is already beginning to rise sullenly from the dark forests. Our pictures show, from the top to the bottom: the Kamnik-Savinja Alps, the Karavanke ridges during sunrise, and two images of the evening colour registers from Kredarica.

On next pages: *The setting sun, impatiently chasing away the moon above Podrta gora in the garland of the Lower Bohinj Mountains. Due to its wild coarseness, precipitous walls and pathlessness, Podrta gora could be called Bohinj lunar country, a hamlet of the elementary beings from space.*

A green and diverse country that lies between the Alps, the Mediterranean, and the Pannonian plain, embraces all the beauties of the Old Continent. If you have ever wished to learn about Europe in one go, Slovenia is the best choice.

Waiting for you are snow-covered mountains and a sea coast caressed by the Mediterranean sun, beautiful karst caves and thermal springs, deep gorges created by clear mountain rivers and wide vistas of slow flatland rivers, mountain lakes and disappearing karst lakes, ancient villages and medieval towns, old castles and modern entertainment centers, innumerable vineyards producing top quality wines, and mysterious primeval forests. Here in Slovenia where hundreds of migrating birds stop at least briefly and where many dozen unique plant and animal species dwell, a variety of experiences seldom to be found elsewhere waits for you all year round.

Slovenia is a land of great natural beauty and a rich cultural and historical heritage. Slovenes and visitors alike are forever discovering new aspects of the country to explore. Slovene tourist farms are oases of peace where city dwellers can spend their vacations in nature and experience the rural way of life. Friendly hosts serve delicious homegrown food and local wines and brandies. You will discover how remarkably beautiful and rich life can be far from the noise of the city.

A millennium has passed since the first castles began to appear in Slovenia. In the first century of their existence, marked by ceaseless feudal struggles, Turkish raids, and peasant rebellions, they were built above steep cliffs, at the top of hills, and in the safety of karst caves, everywhere sillfully exploiting the defensive possibilities of the terrain. As the times became less turbulent, luxurious palaces began to spring up in the cities and powerful manors grew in the valleys, at first in the austere Renaissance style and then in the exuberance of the Baroque period, expanding in their ebullience beyond their walls into wonderful parks.

Truly, Slovenia is a colourful little piece of Europe. Discover it!

Slovenian Tourist Board
www.slovenia-tourism.si

Željko Kozinc, *born 1939, author of the accompanying text, actively works as novelist and screenwriter. Dedicated to journalism since 1959. Awarded a number of highest prizes in the spheres of journalism and screenwriting. Has published five collections of poetry, five novels, a play, The Himalayan Travelogue, and a rich collection of Slovene topographic surveys entitled Nice Day Calling. With his accompanying text, he participated at six photomonographs by Joco Žnidaršič: Photo Joco Žnidaršič, Bohinj, See You at the Market, Golf in Slovenia, Slovenia, the First Ten Years, and the present one. Has written screenplays for seven Slovene feature films, five TV dramas, two documentaries and TV serial about Julius Kugy, for which he received the Austrian National Award. The film Christophoros was proclaimed a winner at the Human Rights Festival in Strasbourg.*

Joco Žnidaršič, *born 1938, author of the photographs, has created numerous photomonographs apart from the present book and has had photographs published in virtually all Slovene newspapers and magazines in the last four decades, due to which he has become one of the leading and most prominent Slovene art and reporter photographers. Among his independent photomonographs let us mention Photo Joco Žnidaršič, Ljubljana, Bohinj, Slovene Vineyards, See you at the Market, Golf in Slovenia, and Slovenia, the first Ten Years, to which the critics responded with high marks and the literary public with a favourable reception. He has contrived and edited seventeen other photomonographs, among which the following have met with the greatest success: The Treasures of Slovenia, The Slovene War, The Beautiful Slovenia, and The Himalayan Travelogue. Joco Žnidaršič is an international master of art photography – EFIAP, and has received more than 50 awards at home and abroad, including World Press Photo and the Prešeren Fund Award – one of the highest Slovene prizes in the sphere of culture.*

Miljenko Licul, *born 1946, designer of the book, works as art director in his own Zodiak Studio. He is particularly well known as designer of the current Slovene coins and bank notes. Has been engaged in design of visual communications since 1968. In 1985 he received, together with Ranko Novak, the Prešeren Fund Award; and was a year later awarded the Plečnik Prize as a member of the group working on Tabor Castle. Has received numerous prizes in the sphere of design. Successfully laid out dozens of books, including the Slovene Chronicle and Nova revija, and five photomonographs by Joco Žnidaršič: appart from this book he has designed Slovene Vineyards, See You at the Market, Golf in Slovenia, and Slovenia, the First Ten Years. Recently, he has also designed the new Slovene passport and some other identification cards.*

Slovenia
My Country

Slovenia – My Country
Photomonography
© Veduta AŽ, d. o. o.

Photographs	Joco Žnidaršič
Introductory text	Milan Kučan
Accompanying text	Željko Kozinc
Layout	Miljenko Licul
Published by	Veduta AŽ, d. o. o.
Publisher represented by	Ana Krajnc Žnidaršič
Translation into English	Henrik Ciglič

Prepress	Delo Repro, d. o. o., Ljubljana
Printed by	Gorenjski tisk, d. d., Kranj
Printed on paper	Larius matt satin 170 gr.,
	Cartiere Burgo S.p.A.,
	Represented by Typographic Stavar

Ljubljana, 2003

CIP – Kataložni zapis o publikaciji
Narodna in univerzitetna knjižnica, Ljubljana

908(497.4)(084.12)
77.047.1(497.4)

ŽNIDARŠIČ, Joco
    Slovenia, my country : [photomonography] /
[photographs] Joco Žnidaršič ; [introductory text Milan Kučan ;
accompanying text Željko Kozinc ; translation into English
Henrik Ciglič]. - Ljubljana : Veduta AŽ, 2002

Izv. nasl.: Moja Slovenija

ISBN 961-90798-9-2

118029312